AFFILLIATE MARKETING

SUCCESSFUL TIPS FOR BEGINNERS

OLUSEGUN SETH AJULO

TABLE OF CONTENT

INTRODUCTION

To begin affiliate marketing, start by selecting a niche you're passionate about. Research affiliate programs within that niche and choose reputable ones. Create quality content to attract your target audience, and incorporate affiliate links naturally. Focus on building trust with your audience, and track your performance using analytics. Experiment, adapt, and refine your strategies as you learn what works best for your audience and niche.

DEFINITION OF AFFILIATE MARKETING

Affiliate marketing is a performance-based online marketing strategy where businesses reward affiliates (partners) for driving traffic or sales to the company's products or services through the affiliate's marketing efforts. Affiliates earn a commission for each successful referral generated through their unique tracking links or codes.

IMPORTANCE OF AFFILIATE MARKETING IN THE DIGITAL AGE

Affiliate marketing is crucial in the digital age for businesses seeking cost-effective ways to reach a broader audience. It allows companies to leverage the online presence of affiliates, tapping into diverse marketing channels and driving targeted traffic. This performance-based model also provides measurable results, enabling businesses to optimize strategies and maximize ROI. Additionally, the collaborative nature of affiliate marketing fosters mutually beneficial relationships between merchants and affiliates, creating a dynamic ecosystem in the digital landscape.

PURPOSE OF THE BOOK: PROVIDING ACTIONABLE TIPS FOR BEGINNERS

The purpose of a book offering actionable tips for beginners is to empower individuals with practical insights and guidance, facilitating their entry into a new subject or skill. By providing tangible, step-by-step advice, the book aims to bridge the gap between theory and application, ensuring readers can readily implement the lessons learned. This approach enhances the learning experience, equipping beginners with the tools they need to take meaningful actions and make tangible progress in their endeavors.

UNDERSTANDING AFFILIATE MARKETING

Affiliate marketing is a performance-based strategy where businesses reward affiliates for driving desired actions, such as sales or leads. Affiliates promote products or services through unique tracking links, earning a commission for each successful referral. It's a cost-effective way for businesses to expand their reach, and for affiliates to monetize their online presence. Successful affiliate marketing involves selecting relevant products, understanding target audiences, and employing effective promotional tactics. The symbiotic relationship between merchants and affiliates makes it a dynamic and mutually beneficial aspect of digital marketing.

EXPLANATION OF AFFILIATE MARKETING CONCEPT

Affiliate marketing involves a partnership between a business (merchant) and individuals or other businesses (affiliates). The affiliate promotes the merchant's products or services through unique tracking links. When customers click on these links and make a purchase or perform a desired action, the affiliate earns a commission. This performance-based model is a win-win: merchants gain increased exposure and sales without upfront costs, while affiliates earn income for driving conversions. The tracking system ensures fair compensation, making affiliate marketing a popular and effective strategy in the digital realm.

KEY PLAYERS: MERCHANTS, AFFILIATES AND CONSUMERS

Key players in affiliate marketing include:

1. Merchants (Advertisers): Businesses that offer products or services and participate in affiliate programs to increase sales and reach a wider audience.

2. Affiliates (Publishers): Individuals or entities that promote the products or services of merchants through various marketing channels and earn commissions for successful referrals.

3. Affiliate Networks: Intermediaries that connect merchants with affiliates, providing a platform for tracking, reporting, and managing affiliate programs efficiently.

4. Customers: The end users who click on affiliate links, making purchases or completing desired actions, ultimately driving revenue for both merchants and affiliates.

5. Affiliate Managers: Individuals or teams responsible for overseeing and optimizing affiliate programs, fostering relationships with affiliates, and ensuring the program's success.

6. Consumers: People who buy products or services through affiliate links, often influenced by the marketing efforts of affiliates.

7. Tracking and Analytics Platforms: Tools and software that help monitor and analyze the performance of affiliate marketing campaigns, providing valuable data for optimization.

Together, these players form a collaborative ecosystem that fuels the success of affiliate marketing programs.

DIFFERENT AFFILIATE MARKETING MODELS

There are several affiliate marketing models, each with its unique structure. Here are some common ones:

1. Pay-Per-Sale (PPS): Affiliates earn a commission when their referral leads to a sale. This model is prevalent in e-commerce.

2. Pay-Per-Lead (PPL): Affiliates receive a commission for generating leads, such as sign-ups or form submissions, for the merchant.

3. Pay-Per-Click (PPC): Affiliates earn a fee based on the number of clicks their referral generates, regardless of whether it results in a sale or lead.

4. Pay-Per-Call (PPC): Affiliates are paid for each phone call made by a customer who clicked on their affiliate link.

5. Two-Tier Affiliate Marketing: Affiliates earn commissions not only for their direct referrals but also for the affiliates they recruit, creating a multi-level commission structure.

6. Multi-Tier Affiliate Marketing: Similar to two-tier, this model involves multiple levels of commissions for affiliates based on the hierarchy of referrals.

7. Revenue Sharing: Affiliates receive a percentage of the revenue generated by the customer they referred, often used in subscription-based services.

8. CPL (Cost Per Lead) or CPA (Cost Per Action): Similar to PPL, affiliates are paid based on a specific action, which could be a sale, lead, or other predetermined actions.

CHOOSING YOUR NICHE

Choosing the right model depends on the goals of the merchant and affiliates, the nature of the product or service, and the target audience.

Choosing a niche involves considering your interests, expertise, and market demand. Start by identifying topics or industries you are passionate about or have knowledge in. Research potential niches to gauge their popularity and competitiveness. Assess the target audience's needs and the potential for profitability. Aim for a balance between your passion and a niche's market viability. Additionally, consider your ability to create valuable content or promote products within that niche. This thoughtful approach increases the likelihood of sustained interest and success in your chosen niche.

IMPORTANCE OF NICHE SELECTION

Niche selection is crucial for several reasons:

1. Targeted Audience: Choosing a niche helps you focus on a specific audience with common interests, making your content or products more appealing to a defined market segment.

2. Expertise and Passion: Selecting a niche aligned with your knowledge or passion enhances your ability to create valuable, authentic content. This enthusiasm often translates into better engagement with your audience.

3. Reduced Competition: Niche markets are often less saturated than broader ones, reducing competition and increasing the chances of standing out as an authority in that specific area.

4. Brand Authority: A well-defined niche allows you to establish yourself as an expert or authority, building trust and credibility within that particular community.

5. Content Relevance: Your content becomes more relevant and resonant when tailored to a specific niche, increasing the likelihood of audience retention and loyalty.

6. Monetization Opportunities: Understanding your niche enables you to identify and capitalize on monetization opportunities, whether through affiliate marketing, product sales, or other revenue streams specific to that market.

7. Marketing Efficiency: Targeting a niche streamlines your marketing efforts, making it easier to reach and connect with your audience through channels that matter most to them.

In essence, niche selection aligns your efforts with a specific audience, allowing for more effective communication, engagement, and potential business success.

RESEARCHING PROFITABLE NICHES

To research profitable niches, consider the following steps:

1. Identify Interests and Expertise: Start by listing your interests, hobbies, and areas of expertise. Choose niches that align with your passion to maintain long-term engagement.

2. Evaluate Market Demand: Use tools like Google Trends, keyword research tools, or market research platforms to assess the demand for potential niches. Look for consistent or growing interest over time.

3. Competitor Analysis: Analyze competitors within your chosen niches. Identify gaps or areas where you can offer unique value. Assess the competition's strengths and weaknesses.

4. Target Audience Research: Understand the needs, problems, and preferences of your target audience. Consider creating buyer personas to guide your niche selection based on audience demographics and behavior.

5. Monetization Potential: Evaluate how you can monetize the niche. Research affiliate programs, potential product offerings, or other revenue streams specific to that market.

6. Check Trends and Seasonality: Examine if the niche is subject to trends or seasonality. A consistent demand throughout the year is generally more favorable for long-term success.

7. Social Media and Online Communities: Explore social media platforms and online communities related to potential niches. Assess the level of engagement and discussions within these communities.

8. Evaluate Your Resources: Consider your ability to create content, products, or services within the niche. Assess the resources required and ensure they align with your capabilities.

9. Legal and Ethical Considerations: Be aware of any legal or ethical considerations associated with the niche. Some industries have specific regulations or standards that may impact your approach.

10. Feedback and Validation: Seek feedback from your network or conduct surveys to validate your chosen niches. This external input can provide valuable insights.

By systematically evaluating these factors, you can identify profitable niches that align with your interests, have market demand, and offer viable monetization opportunities.

EVALUATING YOUR INTERESTS AND EXPERTISE

When evaluating your interests and expertise for niche selection, consider the following:

1. Passion: Identify topics or activities you are genuinely passionate about. Your enthusiasm will fuel your efforts and help you stay committed in the long run.

2. Knowledge and Skills: Assess your existing knowledge and skills. Consider niches where you have expertise or a willingness to learn, as this will contribute to the quality of your content or offerings.

3. Relevance to Audience: Ensure that your interests align with the needs and interests of your target audience. A successful niche bridges the gap between what you love and what your audience finds valuable.

4. Market Demand: Research the market demand for topics related to your interests. Use keyword research tools and trend analysis to gauge the popularity and potential growth of these niches.

5. Competition Analysis: Evaluate the competition within your areas of interest. Look for niches where you can offer a unique perspective or fill a gap in the existing content or products.

6. Monetization Opportunities: Consider how you can monetize your chosen niche. Explore potential affiliate programs, product offerings, or other income streams relevant to your interests and expertise.

7. Long-Term Commitment: Assess your willingness to commit to the niche for the long term. Sustainable success often comes from consistent effort and dedication to your chosen topic.

8. Resource Availability: Evaluate the resources required to create content, products, or services within your chosen niche. Ensure that you have or can acquire the necessary resources to sustain your efforts.

By aligning your interests and expertise with market demand, ensuring relevance to your target audience, and considering the practical aspects of resource availability, you can make informed decisions when selecting a niche. This strategic approach increases the likelihood of long-term success and fulfillment in your chosen endeavors.

ANALYSING MARKET DEMAND AND COMPETITION

When analyzing market demand and competition, follow these steps:

1. Keyword Research: Use tools like Google Keyword Planner, SEMrush, or Ahrefs to identify relevant keywords and gauge search volume. High search volume indicates potential demand.

2. Trend Analysis: Assess the trends related to your chosen niche. Google Trends is a valuable tool to understand the popularity and seasonality of a topic over time.

3. Audience Size and Demographics: Understand the size and demographics of your target audience. Analyze if the niche caters to a broad or specific audience and whether it aligns with your goals.

4. Competitor Research: Identify key competitors within the niche. Analyze their content, products, and marketing strategies. Look for gaps or areas where you can differentiate yourself.

5. SWOT Analysis (Strengths, Weaknesses, Opportunities, Threats): Conduct a SWOT analysis for both your chosen niche and competitors. This helps you understand the internal and external factors influencing your success.

6. Customer Feedback and Reviews: Explore customer reviews and feedback related to products or content within the niche. Understand what customers appreciate and where there might be room for improvement.

7. Social Media Analysis: Monitor social media platforms for discussions and engagement related to the niche. Assess the level of community and interest through likes, shares, and comments.

8. Industry Publications and Reports: Refer to industry publications, reports, or studies relevant to your niche. This can provide insights into market trends, consumer behavior, and potential opportunities.

9. Google Search and Advertisements: Analyze the search engine results and advertisements related to your niche. This can give you an idea of the competition and the types of content or products that perform well.

10. Unique Value Proposition (UVP): Define your unique value proposition. Identify what sets you apart from competitors and how you can fulfill unmet needs in the market.

By thoroughly analyzing market demands and competition, you can make informed decisions about entering a niche. Balancing demand, competition, and your ability to provide unique value is crucial for building a successful presence in any market.

BUILDING YOUR PLATFORM

Building a platform involves creating a strong online presence. Here are key steps:

1. Define Your Brand: Clearly define your brand identity, including your niche, values, and unique selling propositions. This sets the foundation for your platform.

2. Choose a Platform: Decide on the platform(s) you'll use, such as a blog, website, social media channels, or a combination. Each platform serves different purposes, so choose based on your content and audience.

3. Create a Website or Blog: If applicable, set up a website or blog using platforms like WordPress, Wix, or Squarespace. Ensure it's user-friendly, visually appealing, and aligned with your brand.

4. Optimize for SEO: Implement search engine optimization (SEO) techniques to improve your platform's visibility in search results. Use relevant keywords, create quality content, and optimize meta tags.

5. Content Strategy: Develop a content strategy that aligns with your niche and audience. Consistent, valuable content builds credibility and attracts followers.

6. Engage on Social Media: Leverage social media platforms to promote your content, engage with your audience, and build a community. Choose platforms that align with your target audience.

7. Build an Email List: Implement an email marketing strategy to capture and nurture leads. Offer incentives for sign-ups and provide valuable content to your subscribers.

8. Networking: Connect with others in your niche through networking. Collaborate with influencers, participate in forums, and engage with your audience to broaden your reach.

9. Consistent Branding: Maintain consistent branding across all platforms, including visuals, messaging, and tone. This reinforces your identity and makes you easily recognizable.

10. Analytics and Optimization: Use analytics tools to track your platform's performance. Analyze data to understand audience behavior and optimize your strategies accordingly.

11. Monetization Strategies: If your goal is to monetize your platform, explore various strategies such as affiliate marketing, sponsored content, product sales, or memberships.

12. Adapt and Evolve: Stay updated with industry trends and adapt your strategies accordingly. Regularly evaluate your platform's performance and make adjustments as needed.

Building a platform is an ongoing process that requires dedication and adaptability. Focus on providing value, engaging with your audience, and refining your strategies based on feedback and analytics.

CREATING A BLOG OR WEBSITE

Creating a blog or website involves several key steps:

1. Choose a Niche: Select a niche that aligns with your interests, expertise, and potential audience. This will guide your content and attract like-minded visitors.

2. Select a Domain Name: Choose a memorable and relevant domain name for your blog or website. Keep it concise, easy to spell, and reflective of your niche.

3. Register the Domain: Use a domain registrar to register your chosen domain name. Popular registrars include GoDaddy, Namecheap, and Google Domains.

4. Choose a Hosting Provider: Select a reliable hosting provider to host your website. Consider factors like performance, customer support, and pricing. Common choices include Bluehost, SiteGround, and HostGator.

5. Install a Content Management System (CMS): Choose a CMS to manage your website content. WordPress is widely used for its flexibility, ease of use, and extensive community support.

6. Design Your Website: Select a theme or design for your website that complements your content and provides a positive user experience. Customize the design to reflect your brand.

7. Create Essential Pages: Develop essential pages such as Home, About, Contact, and any other relevant pages specific to your content or goals.

8. Set Up Navigation: Organize your website's navigation menu for easy access to different sections. Ensure a logical structure that guides visitors through your content.

9. Install Plugins and Widgets: Enhance functionality with plugins or widgets. For WordPress, plugins can add features like SEO optimization, social media integration, and contact forms.

10. Optimize for SEO: Implement on-page SEO techniques, including keyword optimization, meta tags, and image alt tags. This helps improve your website's visibility in search engine results.

11. Create Quality Content: Start creating and publishing high-quality, valuable content. Consistency is key, so establish a content schedule that suits your capacity.

12. Promote Your Content: Share your content on social media, participate in relevant online communities, and explore other promotional channels to increase visibility.

13. Engage with Your Audience: Respond to comments, encourage discussions, and engage with your audience through social media. Building a community fosters loyalty and repeat visitors.

14. Implement Analytics: Set up analytics tools, such as Google Analytics, to track your website's performance. Analyze data to understand your audience and refine your strategies.

15. Monetization (If Desired): If your goal is to monetize your blog, explore various methods like affiliate marketing, sponsored content, or selling products.

Remember, the success of your blog or website often comes with time, dedication, and continuous improvement. Regularly update content, stay informed about industry trends, and adapt your strategies based on audience feedback and analytics.

CHOOSING A DOMAIN NAME AND HOSTING PROVIDER

Choosing a domain name and hosting provider is a crucial step in creating your online presence. Here are some considerations for each:

Domain Name:

1. Relevance to Niche: Ensure your domain name reflects the theme or focus of your content. It should give visitors an idea of what to expect from your website.

2. Memorability: Opt for a name that is easy to remember. Avoid complex spellings or hyphens that might confuse visitors when typing your URL.

3. Brandable: Aim for a name that is brandable and can contribute to building your online identity. It should be unique and distinguishable.

4. Domain Extension: Choose a suitable domain extension (e.g., .com, .net, .org). While .com is the most common and widely accepted, others can be considered based on availability and relevance.

5. Avoid Trademark Issues: Ensure your chosen domain doesn't infringe on trademarks or copyrights. Check the availability and legality of the name.

6. Future Expansion: Consider the potential for future growth and expansion. The domain should accommodate your long-term goals and any diversification of your content.

Hosting Provider:

1. Reliability and Uptime: Choose a hosting provider with a reputation for reliability and high uptime. Look for reviews and testimonials from other users.

2. Performance: Opt for a hosting plan that provides sufficient resources for your website's needs. Faster loading times contribute to a better user experience.

3. Customer Support: Evaluate the quality and availability of customer support. A responsive support team is essential in case you encounter technical issues.

4. Scalability: Ensure that your hosting plan allows for easy scalability as your website grows. This is crucial for handling increased traffic and resource demands.

5. Security Features: Prioritize hosting providers that offer robust security features, including SSL certificates, firewalls, and regular backups.

6. Ease of Use: Choose a hosting platform with an intuitive interface and easy navigation, especially if you are a beginner. This simplifies the management of your website.

7. Cost: Consider your budget and compare hosting plans. Be aware of any hidden costs and understand the renewal prices after any initial discounts.

8. Reviews and Recommendations: Read reviews and seek recommendations from other website owners. Personal experiences can provide valuable insights into a hosting provider's performance.

Popular hosting providers include Bluehost, SiteGround, and HostGator. Remember that your choice of domain name and hosting provider sets the foundation for your online presence, so take the time to make well-informed decisions.

DESIGNING USER-FRIENDLY INTERFACE

To design a user-friendly interface:

1. Clarity: Ensure clear and concise language, easily understandable icons, and straightforward navigation.

2. Consistency: Maintain uniform design elements, such as colors, fonts, and layout, throughout the interface for a cohesive user experience.

3. Navigation: Create intuitive navigation paths, with easily accessible menus and clear signposts to guide users seamlessly through the app.

4. Feedback: Provide immediate and relevant feedback for user actions to confirm their interactions and assist in error prevention.

5. Hierarchy: Organize information logically with a clear hierarchy, placing important elements prominently and less critical ones accordingly.

6. Whitespace: Use whitespace effectively to avoid clutter, improving readability and allowing users to focus on essential elements.

7. Responsiveness: Ensure the interface responds promptly to user inputs, creating a smooth and satisfying user experience.

8. Accessibility: Design with accessibility in mind, accommodating users with diverse needs by incorporating features like resizable text and screen reader compatibility.

9. User Testing: Regularly conduct usability testing with a diverse group of users to identify and address potential issues.

10. Simplicity: Keep the interface simple and avoid unnecessary complexity, making it easy for users to accomplish tasks without confusion.

Remember, user feedback is crucial for refining and enhancing the interface over time.

LEVERAGING SOCIAL MEDIA PLATFORMS

To leverage social media platforms effectively:

1. Define Goals: Clearly outline your objectives—whether it's brand awareness, engagement, or driving traffic—to tailor your strategy accordingly.

2. Know Your Audience: Understand your target audience on each platform, considering demographics, interests, and behavior to create content that resonates.

3. Consistent Branding: Maintain a consistent brand image across all platforms, including profile pictures, cover photos, and bio information.

4. Content Strategy: Develop a content strategy that aligns with your brand and engages your audience. Use a mix of text, images, videos, and other media types.

5. Posting Schedule: Establish a consistent posting schedule to maintain visibility and engagement. Timing can be crucial, so consider when your audience is most active.

6. Engagement and Interaction: Respond promptly to comments, messages, and mentions. Foster a sense of community by actively engaging with your audience.

7. Visual Appeal: Invest in high-quality visuals to capture attention. Platforms like Instagram and Pinterest rely heavily on visually appealing content.

8. Utilize Features: Take advantage of platform-specific features, such as stories, polls, and live videos, to diversify your content and increase engagement.

9. Analytics and Metrics: Monitor analytics to track the performance of your content. Identify trends, understand what works, and refine your strategy accordingly.

10. Collaborations and Partnerships: Explore collaboration opportunities with influencers or other businesses to expand your reach and tap into new audiences.

Remember, social media is dynamic, so stay adaptable and evolve your strategy based on the changing landscape and user preferences.

UTILIZING FACEBOOK, INSTAGRAM, TWITTER (X), E.T.C.

Here are some platform-specific tips for utilizing Facebook, Instagram, and Twitter(X):

Facebook:

1. Page Optimization: Complete your business page profile with accurate information, a compelling profile picture, and an engaging cover photo.

2. Content Variety: Share a mix of content, including posts, images, videos, and links. Facebook favors diverse content types.

3. Facebook Groups: Join and participate in relevant groups to connect with your target audience and share valuable content.

4. Events: Create and promote events on your page to increase engagement and connect with your audience in real-time.

5. Ads: Utilize Facebook Ads for targeted advertising, allowing you to reach specific demographics and interests.

Instagram:

1. Visual Storytelling: Instagram is highly visual, so focus on compelling visuals that tell a story about your brand.

2. Hashtags: Use relevant and popular hashtags to increase the discoverability of your posts. Create a branded hashtag for your business.

3. Instagram Stories and Reels: Leverage Stories and Reels for engaging, short-form content. Use features like polls and questions to interact with your audience.

4. Collaborations: Partner with influencers or other businesses for shoutouts or takeovers to broaden your reach.

5. Instagram Shopping: If applicable, set up Instagram Shopping to allow users to shop directly from your posts.

Twitter(X):

1. Concise Messaging: Twitter has character limitations, so keep your messages concise and to the point. Use visuals, GIFs, and polls for variety.

2. Hashtags and Trends: Use relevant hashtags and participate in trending topics to increase visibility.

3. Engagement: Respond promptly to mentions and messages. Engage in conversations, retweet relevant content, and participate in Twitter chats.

4. Twitter Lists: Create and subscribe to Twitter Lists to organize and monitor content from specific accounts.

5. Promoted Tweets: Consider using Promoted Tweets for targeted advertising to reach a larger audience.

Remember, each platform has its unique strengths, so tailor your content and strategy accordingly. Regularly analyze performance metrics to refine your approach.

BUILDING AN ENGAGED AUDIENCE

Building an engaged audience requires a strategic and consistent approach. Here are some tips:

1. Know Your Audience: Understand your target audience's interests, preferences, and pain points to create content that resonates with them.

2. Consistent Branding: Maintain a cohesive brand image across all your platforms to build recognition and trust.

3. Content Quality Over Quantity: Focus on creating high-quality, valuable content that addresses your audience's needs. Quality content attracts and retains followers.

4. Regular Posting Schedule: Establish a consistent posting schedule to keep your audience engaged. Timing matters, so consider when your audience is most active.

5. Interact and Respond: Actively engage with your audience by responding to comments, messages, and mentions. Make your audience feel heard and appreciated.

6. Host Giveaways and Contests: Encourage engagement by organizing giveaways or contests. This not only rewards your current audience but also attracts new followers.

7. Use Polls and Surveys: Involve your audience in decision-making through polls and surveys. This not only gathers valuable insights but also increases engagement.

8. Live Sessions and Q&A: Host live sessions or Q&A sessions to connect with your audience in real-time. This creates a sense of community and immediacy.

9. Collaborations and Shout outs: Collaborate with influencers or other businesses to cross-promote and tap into each other's audiences.

10. Exclusive Content: Offer exclusive content or early access to certain information for your loyal followers. This creates a sense of exclusivity and encourages loyalty.

11. Community Building: Foster a sense of community by creating a group or forum where your audience can connect with each other. Actively participate in discussions.

12. Analytics Tracking: Use analytics tools to understand what content performs well. Analyze metrics to refine your strategy based on what resonates with your audience.

Remember, building engagement takes time, so be patient and consistently adapt your approach based on audience feedback and trends.

DEVLOPING AN EMAIL LIST

Building an email list is a valuable strategy for connecting with your audience. Here's a step-by-step guide:

1. Create an Incentive: Offer something of value in exchange for email addresses. This could be a discount, exclusive content, a free resource, or early access to new products/services.

2. Use Opt-in Forms: Place opt-in forms prominently on your website, blog, and social media profiles. Make it easy for visitors to subscribe.

3. Landing Pages: Design dedicated landing pages for specific campaigns or incentives. These pages should focus solely on collecting email addresses.

4. Pop-up Forms: Consider using exit-intent pop-ups or timed pop-ups to capture the attention of website visitors before they leave.

5. Social Media Promotion: Promote your email sign-up across your social media channels. Use compelling visuals and a clear call-to-action.

6. Host Webinars or Events: Require email sign-up for access to webinars or exclusive events. This not only builds your email list but also positions you as an authority in your field.

7. Content Upgrades: Offer content upgrades within your blog posts. This could be additional resources related to the content that readers can receive by providing their email.

8. Referral Programs: Implement a referral program where current subscribers can refer others, creating a viral loop for list growth.

9. Run Contests or Giveaways: Encourage participation in contests or giveaways that require email sign-up. Ensure the prize is relevant to your target audience.

10. Utilize QR Codes: If you have physical locations, use QR codes on printed materials that link to a sign-up form.

11. Segment Your List: As your list grows, segment it based on user preferences, behavior, or demographics. This allows for more targeted and personalized communication.

12. Consistent Communication: Once you have a list, regularly communicate with your subscribers. Provide valuable content, updates, and exclusive offers to keep them engaged.

Always ensure that you have explicit consent from individuals before adding them to your email list to comply with privacy regulations. Regularly clean your list by removing inactive or disengaged subscribers.

CREATING VALUABLE LEAD MAGNETS

Creating valuable lead magnets is essential for attracting and retaining potential customers. Here are some ideas for effective lead magnets:

1. eBooks and Guides: Offer in-depth guides or eBooks that provide valuable insights or solve a specific problem relevant to your audience.

2. Checklists and Cheat Sheets: Create downloadable checklists or cheat sheets that simplify complex processes or offer quick reference guides.

3. Templates and Tools: Provide templates, worksheets, or tools that can save time or enhance productivity in a particular area.

4. Webinars or Online Workshops: Host live or recorded webinars that dive deep into a topic, offering exclusive insights and expertise.

5. Exclusive Reports or Research: Share industry-specific reports, whitepapers, or research findings that are not easily accessible elsewhere.

6. Mini-Courses or Email Series: Break down a complex topic into a series of informative emails or short courses delivered over a few days.

7. Resource Libraries: Build a collection of valuable resources, such as templates, guides, and exclusive content, accessible to subscribers.

8. Free Trials or Samples: Offer a limited-time free trial or sample of your product or service, allowing users to experience its value firsthand.

9. Interactive Quizzes or Assessments: Create engaging quizzes or assessments that provide personalized results or recommendations based on users' responses.

10. Access to a Community or Forum: Grant exclusive access to a community or forum where subscribers can interact, share insights, and learn from each other.

11. Discounts and Special Offers: Provide exclusive discounts or special offers to subscribers, creating a sense of exclusivity and immediate benefit.

12. Case Studies or Success Stories: Share real-life examples of how your product or service has helped others, showcasing the tangible benefits.

Remember to align your lead magnets with your audience's needs and preferences. Prominently feature the value proposition to encourage sign-ups, and ensure a seamless delivery process once users subscribe.

PARTNERING WITH THE RIGHT AFFILIATE PROGRAMS

When choosing affiliate programs to partner with, consider the following factors:

1. Relevance: Ensure the products or services align with your audience and content. This increases the likelihood of conversions.

2. Commission Structure: Compare commission rates and structures. Some programs offer fixed rates, while others may provide a percentage of sales.

3. Cookie Duration: Check the cookie duration, as it determines how long you can earn commissions on a referred customer's purchases.

4. Product Quality: Promote products or services that are reputable and offer value to your audience. This enhances your credibility.

5. Payment Methods: Confirm the payment methods and frequency. Some programs pay monthly, while others have different schedules.

6. Support and Resources: Look for programs that provide adequate support, promotional materials, and resources to help you succeed as an affiliate.

7. Terms and Conditions: Carefully read the affiliate agreement to understand any restrictions or conditions associated with the program.

8. Tracking and Analytics: Choose programs with robust tracking and analytics tools to monitor your performance and optimize your strategy.

RESEARCHING AFFILIATES PROGRAMS

Popular affiliate programs include Amazon Associates, ShareASale, and ClickBank. Tailor your choices to your niche and audience for the best results.

POPULAR AFFILAITES NETWORKS

Certainly! In addition to Amazon Associates and ShareASale, here are some other popular affiliate networks:

1. ClickBank: Known for digital products and a wide range of niches. It's user-friendly and provides detailed statistics.

2. CJ Affiliate (formerly Commission Junction): Offers a diverse range of advertisers and provides advanced reporting tools.

3. Rakuten Marketing: A global network with various brands and products. It's known for its international reach.

4. Awin: Connects affiliates with a variety of advertisers, and it's especially strong in the European market.

5. FlexOffers: Features a vast network of advertisers across different industries with a user-friendly interface.

6. Impact Radius: Provides a comprehensive platform for tracking, managing, and analyzing partnerships.

7. eBay Partner Network: Ideal for affiliates interested in promoting eBay products and earning commissions.

8. PartnerStack: Targets B2B affiliates, connecting them with software and SaaS companies.

Before joining any affiliate network, it's crucial to review their terms, commission structures, and the types of products or services they offer to ensure they align with your audience and content.

ASSESSING COMMISSION RATES AND PAYMENT SCHEDULES

When assessing commission rates and payment schedules for affiliate programs, consider the following:

1. Commission Rates:

   - Compare the commission rates offered by different programs. Some may provide a fixed amount per sale, while others offer a percentage of the sale.

   - Evaluate whether the commission rates are competitive within your niche and industry.

2. Payment Threshold:

   - Check if there is a minimum threshold you need to reach before receiving payments. Some programs only pay out once you've accumulated a certain amount in commissions.

3. Payment Methods:

   - Ensure the affiliate program supports payment methods that are convenient for you. Common methods include bank transfers, PayPal, and checks.

4. Cookie Duration:

   - Understand the cookie duration, as it determines how long you can earn commissions on a customer's purchases after they click on your affiliate link.

5. Recurring Commissions:

   - Some programs offer recurring commissions for subscription-based services. This can lead to long-term income for referred customers.

6. Payment Frequency:

   - Check the payment frequency. Programs may pay monthly, bi-monthly, or on a different schedule. Choose a frequency that aligns with your financial goals and preferences.

7. Terms and Conditions:

   - Review the terms and conditions related to payments. Ensure you understand any hold periods, refund policies, or other factors that may impact your earnings.

8. Performance Bonuses:

   - Some affiliate programs offer performance-based bonuses. Explore whether there are additional incentives for high-performing affiliates.

By carefully considering these factors, you can choose affiliate programs that not only offer competitive commission rates but also align with your preferences and financial goals.

SELECTING PRODUCTS OR SERVICES TO PROMOTE

When selecting products or services to promote as an affiliate, consider the following:

1. Relevance to Your Audience:

   - Choose products or services that resonate with your audience. The more relevant the offering, the higher the likelihood of conversions.

2. Quality and Reputation:

   - Promote products from reputable brands. Quality and a positive reputation contribute to trust and credibility, which can impact your audience's purchasing decisions.

3. Your Personal Experience:

   - If possible, promote products or services you have personal experience with. Your genuine endorsement can be more convincing to your audience.

4. Demand and Popularity:

   - Assess the demand for the products or services. Popular and trending items often have a larger audience, but be mindful of saturation in competitive markets.

5. Commission Structure:

   - Consider the commission rates and structure. Some products may have lower prices but offer higher commission percentages, while others may have higher prices with lower percentages.

6. Affiliate Support:

   - Check if the affiliate program provides adequate support, promotional materials, and resources to help you effectively market the products or services.

7. Conversion Rates:

   - Look for products with good conversion rates. Analyzing historical data or reviews can provide insights into how well a product converts for other affiliates.

8. Seasonal Relevance:

   - Depending on your niche, consider the seasonality of products. Some items may be more relevant or in higher demand during specific times of the year.

9. Ethical Considerations:

   - Ensure that the products or services align with your ethical standards. Promoting items that may be perceived as deceptive or harmful can damage your reputation.

By carefully evaluating these factors, you can choose products or services that not only align with your audience's interests but also contribute to a successful and ethical affiliate marketing strategy.

IDENTIFYING HIGH-CONVERTING PRODUCTS

Identifying high-converting products involves a combination of research, analysis, and understanding your audience. Here are some strategies:

1. Analytics and Data:

   - Use analytics tools to track the performance of different products. Look for those with higher conversion rates, as this indicates they resonate well with your audience.

2. Affiliate Program Insights:

   - Check affiliate program dashboards for metrics such as EPC (earnings per click) and conversion rates. This data can highlight which products are performing well for other affiliates.

3. Customer Reviews and Feedback:

   - Analyze customer reviews and feedback on the products you're considering. Positive experiences can be indicative of products that are likely to convert well.

4. Trends and Seasonal Demand:

   - Stay updated on industry trends and identify products that are currently in demand. Seasonal products may have higher conversion rates during specific times of the year

5. Competitor Analysis:

   - Explore what products similar affiliates in your niche are promoting. While you shouldn't copy directly, it can give you insights into what might be resonating with the audience.

6. Test and Iterate:

   - Conduct A/B testing with different products to understand which ones lead to better conversions. Experiment with variations in your promotional strategies.

7. Product Gravity (For platforms like ClickBank):

   - Some affiliate platforms, like ClickBank, provide a gravity score for products, indicating how well they are selling. Higher gravity often correlates with higher conversions.

8. Social Media and Audience Engagement:

   - Monitor social media engagement and audience discussions. Products that generate excitement or positive conversations may have higher conversion potential.

9. Unique Selling Proposition (USP):

   - Consider products with a unique selling proposition. Products that stand out or offer something distinct may attract more conversions.

Remember, the key is to continuously analyze and adapt based on performance data. High conversion rates may vary across different niches, so understanding your specific audience is crucial for identifying products that resonate with them.

ENSURING RELEVANCE TO YOUR NICHE AND AUDIENCE

Ensuring relevance to your niche and audience is crucial for successful affiliate marketing. Here's how you can maintain that relevance:

1. Understand Your Audience:

   - Develop a deep understanding of your target audience. Know their preferences, needs, and pain points to align with products or services they find valuable.

2. Define Your Niche:

   - Clearly define your niche to attract a specific audience. This helps you tailor your content and promotions to meet the interests of that niche.

3. Content Alignment:

   - Ensure that the products you promote align seamlessly with your content. The transition from your content to the affiliate product should be natural and relevant.

4. Use Case Scenarios:

   - Demonstrate how the affiliate products or services can solve specific problems or enhance the lives of your audience. Real-life use cases make the promotion more relatable.

5. Consistent Messaging:

   - Maintain a consistent message across your content and affiliate promotions. Your audience should recognize a cohesive theme in your recommendations.

6. Integrate Affiliates Organically:

   - Avoid forced or out-of-place promotions. Integrate affiliate recommendations organically into your content to make them feel like genuine endorsements.

7. Regularly Review Products:

   - Periodically review the products or services you promote. Ensure they continue to meet the needs and expectations of your evolving audience.

8. Engage with Your Audience:

   - Actively engage with your audience through comments, surveys, or social media. This interaction provides insights into their evolving preferences.

9. Stay Informed About Industry Trends:

   - Stay updated on trends within your niche. This knowledge helps you identify new and relevant products that align with current interests.

10. Be Transparent:

   - Clearly disclose your affiliate relationships. Transparency builds trust, and your audience will appreciate your honesty about the products you recommend.

By consistently focusing on the needs and preferences of your audience, you can ensure that the products you promote remain relevant to your niche, fostering a stronger connection with your followers.

IMPLEMENTING EFFECTIVE MARKETING STRATEGIES

Implementing effective marketing strategies for affiliate promotion involves a mix of thoughtful planning and execution. Here are key steps:

1. Understand Your Audience:

   - Know your audience's demographics, interests, and behavior. Tailor your strategies to resonate with their preferences.

2. Content Marketing:

   - Create valuable and relevant content that educates, entertains, or solves problems for your audience. Incorporate affiliate links naturally within this content.

3. SEO Optimization:

   - Optimize your content for search engines to attract organic traffic. This includes using relevant keywords and providing valuable information.

4. Email Marketing:

   - Build and nurture an email list. Send targeted emails that provide value and include affiliate promotions strategically.

5. Social Media Engagement:

   - Leverage social media platforms to engage with your audience. Share content, participate in discussions, and promote affiliate products where appropriate.

6. Paid Advertising:

   - Consider paid advertising channels such as Google Ads or social media ads. Target specific demographics to maximize the impact of your campaigns.

7. In-depth Product Reviews:

   - Create comprehensive reviews of the products or services you're promoting. Include both pros and cons to provide an honest assessment.

8. Use Visual Content:

   - Incorporate visual elements such as images, infographics, or videos to make your content more engaging. Visuals can enhance the appeal of affiliate products.

9. Leverage Webinars or Live Sessions:

   - Host webinars or live sessions to interact with your audience in real-time. Use these opportunities to showcase affiliate products and answer questions.

10. Test and Analyze:

   - Continuously test different strategies to see what works best for your audience. Use analytics to measure the performance of your campaigns and adjust accordingly.

11. Build Trust:

   - Establish trust with your audience by being transparent, providing valuable content, and recommending products genuinely beneficial to them.

12. Diversify Platforms:

   - Spread your affiliate promotions across various platforms. Don't rely solely on one channel; diversification can help you reach a broader audience.

13. Stay Updated on Trends:

   - Keep abreast of industry trends and adjust your strategies accordingly. Staying current ensures your approach remains effective.

Remember, successful marketing strategies often involve a combination of these tactics. Tailor your approach based on your audience, the products you're promoting, and the platforms you're using. Regularly assess your performance and be willing to adapt to changing circumstances.

CONTENT MARKETING TECHNIQUES

Effective content marketing involves creating valuable, relevant content to attract and engage your target audience. Here are some techniques:

1. Understand Your Audience: Know your target audience's needs, preferences, and pain points to create content that resonates.

2. Keyword Research: Use SEO tools to identify relevant keywords and incorporate them naturally into your content for better search engine visibility.

3. Quality Content: Create high-quality, informative, and shareable content that addresses your audience's problems or provides valuable insights.

4. Consistency: Maintain a consistent publishing schedule to keep your audience engaged and build trust over time.

5. Visual Content: Incorporate visuals like images, infographics, and videos to enhance engagement and convey information more effectively.

6. Storytelling: Tell compelling stories to connect emotionally with your audience, making your content memorable and relatable.

7. Promotion: Actively promote your content through social media, email marketing, and other channels to reach a wider audience.

8. Interactive Content: Experiment with quizzes, polls, surveys, and other interactive formats to increase user engagement.

9. Guest Posting: Contribute content to reputable websites in your industry to expand your reach and build authority.

10. Analytics: Use analytics tools to track the performance of your content, understand what works, and make data-driven improvements.

11. Email Marketing: Build and nurture your email list by providing valuable content, and use email campaigns to stay connected with your audience.

12. Content Upgrades: Offer additional resources or exclusive content as incentives for visitors to subscribe to your newsletter or take specific actions.

13. User-generated Content: Encourage your audience to create and share content related to your brand, fostering community and increasing reach.

14. Podcasting: Consider creating a podcast to reach audiences who prefer audio content and build a loyal listener base.

15. Adapt to Trends: Stay updated on industry trends and adapt your content strategy to incorporate new formats or platforms.

Remember, the key is to provide value to your audience consistently and adapt your strategy based on their preferences and changing trends.

WRITING COMPELLING PRODUCT REVIEWS

Crafting compelling product reviews can influence potential buyers and provide valuable information. Here's a guide:

1. Know Your Audience: Tailor your review to the needs and preferences of your target audience. Consider what they value in a product.

2. Use the Product: Provide an authentic review by using the product yourself. Share your personal experiences, both positive and negative.

3. Clear Structure: Organize your review with a clear structure - introduction, features, pros and cons, your experience, and a conclusion.

4. Catchy Title: Create a title that grabs attention and gives a hint of what the review is about. Use adjectives to evoke interest.

5. Engaging Introduction: Start with a captivating introduction to hook your readers. State the problem the product solves or highlight its unique selling proposition.

6. Details and Features: List the key features of the product and explain how each contributes to its overall performance or user experience.

7. Personal Experience: Share your personal journey with the product. Discuss how it met or exceeded your expectations and if there were any surprises.

8. Pros and Cons: Be honest about both the strengths and weaknesses of the product. This builds trust with your audience.

9. Use Descriptive Language: Paint a vivid picture with your words. Instead of saying "good," use specific adjectives like "durable," "versatile," or "efficient."

10. Include Multimedia: Add images or videos to visually showcase the product. This helps your audience visualize the item in action.

11. Comparison: If applicable, compare the product to similar ones in the market. Highlight what sets it apart and why it might be a better choice.

12. Address Concerns: Anticipate common questions or concerns your audience might have and address them in your review.

13. Call to Action: Conclude your review with a clear call to action. This could be encouraging readers to make a purchase, share their thoughts, or ask questions.

14. SEO Optimization: Use relevant keywords naturally in your review to enhance its visibility in search engine results.

15. Honesty is Key: Maintain honesty throughout your review. Readers appreciate authenticity, and it helps establish your credibility as a reviewer.

Remember, your goal is to help your audience make informed decisions. A well-crafted, honest review can build trust and influence purchasing choices.

CREATING ENGAGING AND INFORMATIVE CONTENT

To create engaging and informative content, consider the following tips:

1. Know Your Audience: Understand your target audience's preferences, needs, and pain points to tailor your content to resonate with them.

2. Clear Purpose: Define the purpose of your content. Whether it's to educate, entertain, or inspire, having a clear goal will guide your writing.

3. Compelling Headlines: Craft attention-grabbing headlines that spark curiosity and encourage readers to delve into your content.

4. Introduction Matters: Capture your audience's attention from the start. Use a compelling introduction that sets the tone and promises value.

5. Use Visuals: Incorporate visually appealing elements like images, infographics, and videos to enhance the overall experience and convey information effectively.

6. Break it Down: Use short paragraphs, subheadings, and bullet points to break down complex information, making it easy for readers to digest.

7. Storytelling: Weave stories into your content to make it relatable and memorable. People connect emotionally with stories.

8. Engage with Questions: Pose questions to your audience within the content to encourage interaction and make them think.

9. Include Data and Examples: Support your points with relevant data and real-world examples. This adds credibility and depth to your content.

10. Personalize the Tone: Adopt a conversational tone to make your content more approachable. Imagine you're having a one-on-one conversation with your audience.

11. Keep it Relevant: Ensure your content is timely and addresses current trends or issues in your industry. This keeps it relevant and valuable.

12. Provide Solutions Identify problems your audience faces and offer practical solutions. This positions your content as genuinely helpful.

13. Call to Action (CTA): Clearly state what you want your audience to do after consuming the content. Whether it's sharing, commenting, or taking a specific action, guide them.

14. Optimize for Readability: Use a readable font, appropriate font size, and consider the use of whitespace to enhance the overall readability of your content.

15. Interactive Elements: Incorporate polls, quizzes, or other interactive elements to keep your audience engaged and encourage participation.

By combining these elements, you can create content that not only informs but also captivates your audience, fostering a stronger connection and encouraging them to take the desired actions.

SEARCH ENGINE OPTIMIZATION (SEO)

Search Engine Optimization (SEO) is crucial for improving a website's visibility on search engines. Here are key aspects to consider:

1. Keyword Research: Identify relevant keywords related to your content and industry. Use tools to find keywords with high search volume and low competition.

2. On-Page Optimization:

   -Title Tags: Craft compelling and concise title tags for each page, incorporating relevant keywords.

   - Meta Descriptions: Write informative meta descriptions that encourage users to click, also including relevant keywords.

   - Header Tags: Use headers (H1, H2, H3) to structure your content, making it easier for both users and search engines to understand.

3. Quality Content: Create high-quality, valuable content that addresses users' needs. Google prioritizes content that provides genuine value.

4. Mobile-Friendly Design: Ensure your website is mobile-friendly, as mobile usability is a significant factor in search engine rankings.

5. Page Loading Speed: Optimize your site's loading speed. Use compressed images, minimize HTTP requests, and leverage browser caching to improve performance.

6. Internal Linking: Connect relevant pages within your website through internal links. This helps distribute authority and guides users to related content.

7. Backlinks: Earn high-quality backlinks from reputable websites. Quality matters more than quantity; focus on natural link-building.

8. User Experience (UX): Prioritize a positive user experience. An easy-to-navigate site with clear calls-to-action enhances user satisfaction.

9. Schema Markup: Implement schema markup to provide additional context to search engines, improving the way your content appears in search results.

10. Social Signals: While not a direct ranking factor, social media activity can contribute to your website's visibility. Share your content on social platforms to increase its reach.

11. Regular Updates: Keep your content up-to-date. Google prefers fresh and relevant content, and regularly updated pages may rank higher.

12. Local SEO: If applicable, optimize for local search by claiming and updating your Google My Business listing. Ensure consistency in your business information across online platforms.

13. Analytics: Use tools like Google Analytics to track your website's performance. Monitor key metrics such as traffic, bounce rate, and conversions.

14. SSL Certificate: Secure your website with an SSL certificate. Google gives preference to secure sites, and it improves user trust.

15. Compliance with Web Standards Adhere to web standards and best practices. This includes proper HTML structure, avoiding duplicate content, and creating a sitemap.

SEO is an ongoing process, and staying informed about algorithm updates and industry trends is crucial for long-term success. Regularly audit and update your SEO strategy to adapt to changes in search engine algorithms and user behavior.

KEYWORD RESEARCH AND OPTIMIZATION

Keyword research and optimization are crucial components of a successful SEO strategy. Here's a guide to help you navigate these aspects:

Keyword Research:

1. Understand Your Niche:

   - Identify the main topics and themes related to your business or content.

2. Brainstorm Seed Keywords:

   - Create a list of broad, general keywords that represent your niche.

3. Use Keyword Research Tools:

   - Utilize tools like Google Keyword Planner, SEMrush, or Ahrefs to find relevant keywords.

   - Look for keywords with a balance of search volume and competition.

4. Long-Tail Keywords:

   - Include long-tail keywords (more specific, longer phrases) to capture targeted traffic.

5. Competitor Analysis:

   - Analyze competitors' websites to discover the keywords they are targeting.

6. User Intent:

   - Understand the intent behind the search queries (informational, transactional, navigational) and align your content accordingly.

7. Local Keywords:

   - If applicable, include location-based keywords to enhance local SEO.

Keyword Optimization:

8. Primary Keyword Placement:

   - Place your primary keyword in the page title, meta description, and headings (H1, H2) for on-page optimization.

9. Content Optimization:

   - Integrate keywords naturally into your content, ensuring readability and relevance.

   - Avoid keyword stuffing; prioritize user experience.

10. URL Structure:

   - Incorporate keywords into your URL structure. Keep it short, descriptive, and user-friendly.

11. Image Alt Text:

   - Optimize image alt text with relevant keywords to enhance accessibility and provide context to search engines.

12. Internal Linking

   - Use internal links with anchor text that includes relevant keywords to improve page connections.

13. Backlink Anchor Text:

   - When earning backlinks, encourage anchor text that includes your target keywords. However, ensure it looks natural.

14. Header Tags:

   - Use header tags (H1, H2, etc.) to structure your content, incorporating keywords where relevant.

15. Regularly Update Content:

   - Keep your content fresh and updated with the latest information, including new keywords if necessary.

16. Monitor and Adjust:

   - Regularly check the performance of your keywords using analytics tools. Adjust your strategy based on changing trends and user behavior.

17. Create Cornerstone Content:

  - Develop comprehensive, authoritative content around your primary keywords to establish your expertise.

18. Mobile Optimization:

  - Ensure your website is mobile-friendly, as mobile searches are increasingly prevalent.

19. Meta Tags:

  - Craft compelling meta titles and descriptions, including keywords to entice clicks from search engine results pages (SERPs).

Remember, the goal is not just to rank for keywords but to provide valuable content that aligns with user intent. Continuously refine your keyword strategy based on performance data and industry changes.

BUILDING HIGH-QUALITY BACKLINKS

Building high-quality backlinks is a crucial aspect of SEO that requires a strategic and ethical approach. Here are effective ways to acquire quality backlinks:

1. Create High-Quality Content:

  - Develop content that is valuable, unique, and relevant to your target audience. Quality content naturally attracts links.

2. Guest Blogging:

  - Contribute guest posts to reputable websites in your industry. Ensure the content is valuable and aligns with the host site's audience.

3. Broken Link Building:

  - Identify broken links on authoritative websites in your niche and reach out to suggest your content as a replacement.

4. Skyscraper Technique:

   - Find popular content in your niche, create something even more valuable, and then reach out to sites that linked to the original content.

5. Build Relationships:

   - Cultivate relationships with influencers, bloggers, and other content creators in your industry. Networking can lead to organic backlinks.

6. Infographics:

   - Create visually appealing infographics and share them on your site. Infographics are highly shareable and can attract backlinks.

7. Linkable Assets:

   - Develop linkable assets such as in-depth guides, research, or tools that others in your industry would want to reference and link to.

8. Testimonials:

   - Provide testimonials for products or services you've used. Some businesses may include a link back to your site when featuring your testimonial.

9. Social Media Promotion:

   - Actively promote your content on social media to increase its visibility. Increased visibility can lead to more backlink opportunities.

10. Participate in Communities:

   - Engage in online communities, forums, and discussion platforms related to your niche. Share your expertise, and if allowed, include links to relevant content.

11. Resource Pages:

   - Identify resource pages in your industry and reach out to be included. Ensure your content adds value to the page.

12. Haro (Help a Reporter Out):

   - Sign up for HARO and respond to relevant queries from journalists. If your response gets featured, you may earn a high-quality backlink.

13.Local Business Directories:

   - Ensure your business is listed on reputable local directories. This not only helps with SEO but also provides valuable backlinks.

14. Collaborate on Projects:

   - Collaborate with other businesses or influencers on joint projects. This could be a co-authored piece of content, an event, or a webinar.

15. Ego Bait:

   - Create content that highlights and praises influencers or businesses in your industry. They may link to or share the content.

Remember, the key is to focus on quality rather than quantity. Building a natural and diverse backlink profile over time is more effective than pursuing shortcuts that violate search engine guidelines. Regularly monitor your backlink profile and disavow any low-quality or spammy links that could harm your SEO.

PAID ADVERTISING OPTIONS

GOOGLE ADS, SOCIAL MEDIA ADS E.T.C.

In affiliate marketing, paid advertising can be an effective strategy. Some options include:

1. Google Ads: Create targeted campaigns to reach potential customers searching for related products or services.

2. Facebook Ads: Utilize Facebook's detailed targeting options to reach a specific audience based on demographics, interests, and behavior.

3. Instagram Ads: Leverage visually appealing content to promote affiliate products on Instagram, which is owned by Facebook.

4. Native Advertising: Blend ads seamlessly with the content on a platform to make them appear more organic and less intrusive.

5. YouTube Ads: Create engaging video content to promote affiliate products through YouTube's advertising platform.

6. LinkedIn Ads: If your target audience is in the professional sphere, use LinkedIn to promote affiliate products.

7. Twitter Ads: Promote affiliate offers through promoted tweets to reach a wider audience on Twitter.

When using paid advertising in affiliate marketing, it's crucial to comply with the policies of the advertising platform and clearly disclose your affiliate relationships to maintain transparency with your audience.

BUDGETING AND TRACKING ROI

Budgeting involves setting financial limits for various activities, while tracking ROI (Return on Investment) assesses the profitability of those investments. Use tools like spreadsheets to create a budget, and regularly analyze financial reports to evaluate ROI, ensuring effective resource allocation.

TRACKING AND ANALYISING PERFORMANCE

To track and analyze performance in affiliate marketing, use tools like Google Analytics, track affiliate links with UTM parameters, monitor conversion rates, and analyze affiliate network reports. Regularly review data to optimize campaigns and identify high-performing channels.

Analytics in affiliate marketing is crucial for several reasons:

1. Performance Measurement: Analytics tools help track key metrics such as clicks, conversions, and revenue, allowing affiliates to gauge the success of their campaigns.

2. ROI Analysis: By analyzing data, affiliates can calculate their return on investment (ROI), helping them understand which campaigns are profitable and where adjustments are needed.

3. Targeted Optimization: Analytics reveal which marketing channels and strategies are most effective, enabling affiliates to optimize their efforts for better results.

4. Audience Insights: Understanding audience behavior through analytics helps affiliates tailor their approach, ensuring that promotional efforts align with the preferences and interests of their target audience.

5. Budget Allocation: Analytics assist in allocating resources wisely by identifying top-performing campaigns, allowing affiliates to focus their budget on activities that generate the highest returns.

6. Fraud Detection: Tracking analytics can help identify fraudulent activities or suspicious patterns, allowing affiliates to take preventive measures and protect their commissions.

7. Continuous Improvement: Regularly analyzing data allows affiliates to adapt to market trends, refine their strategies, and continuously improve their performance in the dynamic affiliate marketing landscape.

In summary, analytics provides valuable insights that empower affiliates to make informed decisions, optimize their campaigns, and ultimately enhance their overall effectiveness in the affiliate marketing space

IMPORTANCE OF ANALYTICS IN AFFILIATE MARKETING

Analytics play a crucial role in affiliate marketing for several reasons:

1. Performance Measurement: Analytics tools help track the performance of affiliate campaigns, providing insights into key metrics such as clicks, conversions, and revenue. This data allows marketers to assess the success of their efforts.

2. ROI Calculation: By analyzing data on conversions and associated revenue, affiliates can calculate their return on investment (ROI). This information is essential for optimizing campaigns and focusing efforts on the most lucrative avenues.

3. Audience Insights: Analytics provide valuable information about the audience engaging with affiliate content. Understanding demographics, interests, and behavior helps tailor marketing strategies to target specific audience segments more effectively.

4. Tracking Conversions: Accurate tracking through analytics enables affiliates to attribute conversions to specific marketing channels, campaigns, or even individual creatives. This insight aids in refining strategies and allocating resources wisely.

5. Adapting Strategies: Regular analysis allows affiliates to adapt their strategies based on performance trends. Identifying what works and what doesn't helps refine approaches and maximize the impact of marketing efforts.

6. Compliance Monitoring: Analytics tools assist in monitoring compliance with affiliate program terms and conditions. This includes ensuring that promotional methods align with the guidelines set by merchants and affiliate networks.

7. Decision Making: Informed decision-making relies on data. Analytics empower affiliates to make strategic decisions by providing a comprehensive understanding of campaign performance, helping them allocate resources efficiently.

8. Optimizing Campaigns: Through ongoing analysis, affiliates can identify underperforming aspects of their campaigns and make necessary adjustments. This might involve tweaking ad creatives, adjusting targeting parameters, or experimenting with different promotional channels.

In essence, analytics are a fundamental component of successful affiliate marketing, providing the data-driven insights needed to refine strategies, enhance performance, and ultimately achieve better results.

UTILIZING TRACKING TOOLS AND SOFTWARES

Effective utilization of tracking tools and software is essential in affiliate marketing for optimizing performance and maximizing returns. Here's how you can make the most of them:

1. Implement Tracking Pixels: Use tracking pixels to monitor user actions on your website. This allows you to gather data on conversions, click-through rates, and other critical metrics.

2. UTM Parameters: Add UTM parameters to your affiliate links. This helps in identifying the source of traffic, allowing for detailed analysis of the performance of different marketing channels.

3. Conversion Tracking: Utilize conversion tracking tools to measure the success of specific actions, such as completed purchases. This insight is invaluable for assessing the effectiveness of your affiliate campaigns.

4. Affiliate Network Tools: Leverage the tracking tools provided by affiliate networks. These tools often offer detailed reports on clicks, impressions, and commissions, aiding in performance analysis.

5. Google Analytics: Integrate Google Analytics to gain comprehensive insights into user behavior, traffic sources, and audience demographics. This data can inform strategic decisions and optimizations.

6. Heatmaps and Session Recording: Employ tools that provide heatmaps and session recording. This visual data allows you to understand how users interact with your site, helping you enhance user experience and identify potential issues.

7. Fraud Prevention Tools: Use tools designed to detect and prevent affiliate fraud. Protecting your campaigns from fraudulent activities ensures that your marketing budget is used efficiently.

8. A/B Testing Tools: Implement A/B testing tools to experiment with different creatives, landing pages, or promotional strategies. This helps in identifying the most effective elements for maximizing conversions.

9. Real-time Analytics: Choose tools that offer real-time analytics. This allows you to react promptly to changes in campaign performance and make immediate adjustments for better results.

10. Custom Dashboards: Create customized dashboards in your tracking software to focus on the specific metrics that matter most to your affiliate marketing goals. This streamlines your analysis process.

By integrating and actively using these tracking tools, you can gather actionable insights, optimize your affiliate campaigns, and ultimately improve your overall performance in the competitive landscape of affiliate marketing.

ANALYSING CLICK-THROUGH RATES, CONVERSION RATES, AND COMMISSIONS EARNED

To analyze click-through rates (CTR), conversion rates, and commission earned, you'll want to assess the performance of your online content or marketing efforts. High CTR indicates effective ad or content engagement, while conversion rates measure the percentage of users taking desired actions. Commission earned depends on successful conversions.

1. Click-Through Rates (CTR)

  - Calculate CTR: (Number of clicks / Number of impressions) * 100.

  - High CTR suggests your content is enticing. Low CTR may indicate the need for more compelling headlines or visuals.

2. Conversion Rates:

  - Calculate Conversion Rate: (Number of conversions / Number of clicks) * 100.

- A high conversion rate means a good proportion of clicks lead to desired actions. Low rates may indicate issues with the landing page or call-to-action.

3. Commission Earned:

  - Assess commission earnings based on successful conversions.

  - Look at the overall revenue generated and evaluate if it aligns with your goals and expectations.

Consider using analytics tools like Google Analytics or platform-specific tools to gather detailed insights. Regularly monitor and tweak your strategies based on the performance metrics to optimize for better results.

MAKING DATA-DRIVEN DECISIONS TO OPTIMIZE STRATEGIES

Analyzing relevant data allows you to identify patterns, trends, and insights, enabling informed decision-making to optimize strategies. Utilize key metrics, measure performance, and adapt strategies based on data-driven insights for continuous improvement

1. Ignoring Product Quality: Promoting low-quality products can harm your reputation and credibility.

2. Overlooking Disclosure: Failing to disclose affiliate relationships may violate regulations and erode trust with your audience.

3. Not Testing Products: Endorsing products without testing them may lead to promoting ineffective or unreliable items.

4. Neglecting Target Audience: Understanding your audience is crucial; promoting irrelevant products can result in low conversion rates.

5. Ignoring Analytics: Neglecting to track and analyze performance metrics can hinder your ability to optimize and improve your strategy.

6. Relying Solely on SEO: Diversify your traffic sources; relying solely on SEO can make your strategy vulnerable to algorithm changes.

7. Misleading Content: Providing inaccurate information or making false claims can damage your reputation and lead to legal issues.

8. Ignoring Trends: Staying updated with industry trends helps you adapt your strategy to changing market dynamics.

9. Not Building an Email List: Failing to capture leads means missing out on long-term engagement and potential sales.

10. Choosing Low-Commission Products: Prioritize products with reasonable commissions to ensure your efforts are adequately rewarded.

If you're experiencing affiliate marketing burnout, consider reassessing your priorities, setting realistic goals, and taking breaks to recharge. Diversify your tasks, automate where possible, and focus on activities that bring joy and results. Seeking support from peers or mentors can also provide valuable perspectives.

OVERCOMING CHALLENGES AND PITFALLS

Rejection and setbacks are common in affiliate marketing. Stay resilient by analyzing what went wrong, adjusting your strategy, and learning from the experience. Building relationships with your audience and refining your approach can turn setbacks into opportunities for growth.

COMMON MISTAKES TO AVOID

In affiliate marketing, learning from failures is crucial. Analyze unsuccessful campaigns, identify what went wrong, and adapt your strategies accordingly. This iterative process helps refine your approach, optimize targeting, and enhance overall performance over time.

DEALING WITH AFFILIATE MARKETING BURNOUT

Dealing with affiliate marketing burnout is crucial for maintaining long-term success. Here are some strategies to help:

1. Set Realistic Goals: Establish achievable and realistic short-term and long-term goals. This prevents the feeling of overwhelm and allows you to celebrate smaller victories along the way.

2. Diversify Strategies: Avoid relying heavily on a single marketing channel or product. Diversifying your efforts can make the work more interesting and reduce the impact of fluctuations in one area.

3. Take Breaks: Schedule regular breaks to recharge. Stepping away from your work, even for short periods, can improve focus and prevent burnout.

4. Evaluate Workload Assess your workload and prioritize tasks. Delegate or eliminate non-essential activities that contribute to stress without significant value.

5. Learn to Say No: Don't overcommit. Saying no to additional projects or partnerships when you're already stretched thin is essential for maintaining a healthy work-life balance.

6. Mindful Relaxation Techniques: Incorporate relaxation techniques such as deep breathing, meditation, or mindfulness into your routine. These practices can help alleviate stress and improve mental well-being.

7. Connect with Peers: Join affiliate marketing communities or networks where you can connect with peers. Sharing experiences, challenges, and solutions can provide valuable support and insights.

8. Reassess and Adjust: Regularly reassess your strategies and adjust as needed. Markets and trends evolve, and staying adaptable can help prevent burnout by keeping your approach fresh and effective.

9. Seek Professional Help: If burnout persists, consider seeking guidance from a mentor or professional coach. They can provide valuable perspectives and strategies to navigate challenges.

10. Personal Time: Prioritize personal time and hobbies. Balancing work with activities you enjoy is essential for overall well-being and helps prevent burnout.

Remember, burnout is a common challenge in any demanding field, including affiliate marketing. Taking proactive steps to manage stress and maintain a healthy work-life balance is key to sustaining long-term success.

HANDLING REJECTION AND SETBACKS

Handling rejection and setbacks is a crucial skill in any field, including affiliate marketing. Here are some strategies to cope with them:

1. Maintain Perspective: Remember that rejection is not a reflection of your worth or abilities. It's a natural part of any business or creative endeavor.

2. Learn from Setbacks: Instead of dwelling on failures, view them as opportunities for learning and growth. Analyze what went wrong, identify areas for improvement, and use setbacks as stepping stones toward success.

3. Stay Positive: Cultivate a positive mindset. Focus on your strengths, achievements, and the progress you've made. Optimism can help you bounce back from setbacks more resiliently.

4. Seek Feedback: If possible, seek constructive feedback from those who rejected your proposal or campaign. Understanding their perspective can provide valuable insights for improvement.

5. Adjust Expectations: Set realistic expectations and understand that not every opportunity will result in success. Adjusting expectations can help reduce the impact of rejection.

6. Keep Moving Forward: Don't let setbacks paralyze you. Keep moving forward by setting new goals and focusing on the next opportunity. Persistence often leads to success.

7. Build Resilience: Develop resilience by acknowledging that setbacks are part of the journey. Resilient individuals bounce back from failures with renewed determination.

8. Celebrate Small Wins: Acknowledge and celebrate small achievements along the way. Recognizing progress, no matter how minor, can boost morale and motivation.

9. Network and Support: Surround yourself with a supportive network. Share your experiences with peers or mentors who can offer guidance, encouragement, and a fresh perspective.

10. Self-Care: Take care of your physical and mental well-being. Exercise, proper nutrition, and sufficient rest contribute to resilience and the ability to navigate challenges effectively.

Remember, rejection and setbacks are inherent in any entrepreneurial or marketing venture. They are not indicators of permanent failure but rather opportunities for growth and improvement. Embracing a positive and resilient mindset can be a powerful tool in your journey toward success.

LEARNING FROM FAILURES AND ADAPTING STRATEGIES

Learning from failures is a crucial aspect of growth in any field, including affiliate marketing. Here's how you can effectively learn from setbacks and adapt your strategies:

1. Reflect on Failure: Take the time to reflect on what went wrong. Analyze the situation objectively, identifying specific factors that contributed to the failure.

2. Identify Lessons: Extract lessons from the failure. Understand what worked and what didn't. This analysis can provide valuable insights that will shape your future strategies.

3. Adjust Mindset: Adopt a growth mindset. See failures as opportunities for learning and improvement rather than as insurmountable obstacles. This perspective shift can fuel resilience and innovation.

4. Seek Feedback: If possible, seek feedback from peers, mentors, or those involved in the situation. External perspectives can provide additional insights that may not be immediately apparent.

5. Prioritize Adaptability: Embrace adaptability as a core trait. The ability to adjust strategies based on lessons learned is a key component of long-term success in affiliate marketing.

6. Set Realistic Goals: Use the lessons learned to set more realistic and achievable goals. Adjust your expectations while maintaining ambition, ensuring that your goals align with your capabilities and resources.

7. Test and Iterate: Implement changes gradually, testing new strategies and monitoring their impact. Continuous iteration allows you to refine your approach based on real-world feedback.

8. Diversify Strategies: If a particular approach failed, consider diversifying your strategies. Explore different marketing channels, audience segments, or product categories to spread risk and increase opportunities for success.

9. Stay Informed: Keep abreast of industry trends, updates, and changes. Staying informed allows you to proactively adapt your strategies to align with the evolving landscape of affiliate marketing.

10. Celebrate Successes: When you implement changes and see positive results, celebrate those successes. Acknowledge the progress you've made and use it as motivation to continue refining your strategies.

Remember, failure is not the end but a stepping stone toward improvement. Embrace the iterative nature of affiliate marketing, where each failure brings you closer to a more refined and effective approach.

SCALING YOUR AFFILIATE MARKETING BUSINESS

To scale your affiliate marketing business, focus on these key strategies:

1. Diversify Products and Niches:

  - Expand your offerings to target a broader audience.

  - Explore different niches to tap into various markets.

2. Optimize Content and SEO:

   - Create high-quality, SEO-optimized content to improve search engine rankings.

   - Use relevant keywords to attract organic traffic.

3. Build an Email List:

   - Capture leads through opt-in forms on your website.

   - Nurture your email list with valuable content and affiliate offers.

4. Social Media Marketing:

   - Leverage social platforms to promote your affiliate products.

   - Engage with your audience and share content that drives traffic.

5.Paid Advertising:

   - Invest in targeted paid advertising to reach a wider audience.

   - Utilize platforms like Google Ads or social media ads strategically.

6. Data Analytics:

   - Use analytics tools to track performance and identify successful channels.

   - Optimize campaigns based on data to maximize ROI.

7. Partner with Influencers:

   - Collaborate with influencers in your niche for wider reach.

   - Influencers can introduce your products to their engaged audience.

8. Automate and Outsource:

   - Implement automation tools for repetitive tasks.

   - Consider outsourcing non-core activities to focus on growth strategies.

9. Stay Updated on Trends:

   - Keep abreast of industry trends and adapt your strategy accordingly.

   - Embrace new technologies and marketing techniques.

10. Customer Relationship Management (CRM):

   - Implement a CRM system to manage and nurture relationships with customers.

   - Enhance customer satisfaction for repeat business.

Remember, consistency and adaptability are crucial for long-term success in affiliate marketing.

OUTSOURCING TASKS TO SCALE YOUR OPERATIONS

Outsourcing tasks can significantly enhance scalability. Here's how:

1. Identify Repetitive Tasks:

   - Pinpoint tasks that are time-consuming but don't necessarily require your direct involvement.

2. Choose Reliable Partners:

   - Select reputable outsourcing partners or freelancers with proven track records.

3. Define Clear Objectives:

   - Clearly communicate your expectations and objectives to ensure alignment with outsourced tasks.

4. Cost-Effective Solutions:

   - Outsource tasks that can be done more cost-effectively by external experts, freeing up resources.

5. Technology Integration:

   - Leverage technology tools to facilitate communication and collaboration with remote teams.

6. Data Security Measures:

   - Implement robust data security measures to protect sensitive information when outsourcing.

7. Continuous Communication:

   - Maintain open lines of communication to address concerns promptly and ensure smooth collaboration.

8. Training and Guidelines:

   - Provide thorough training and guidelines to ensure outsourced teams understand your business processes.

9. Scalability Planning:

   - Choose outsourcing partners that can scale their services according to your growing needs.

10. Focus on Core Competencies:

   - Direct your attention to core business functions while outsourcing routine tasks to experts.

11. Quality Control:

   - Establish quality control measures to maintain the standard of work delivered by outsourcing partners.

12. Legal Agreements:

   - Draft clear and comprehensive contracts to define terms, expectations, and responsibilities.

By outsourcing non-core tasks, you can optimize your time, reduce operational costs, and focus on strategic aspects of your business, contributing to overall scalability

EXPANDING TO NEW NICHES OR PRODUCTS

Expanding to new niches or products can fuel business growth. Consider these steps:

1. Market Research:

  - Conduct thorough market research to identify viable niches or products.

  - Understand customer needs, competition, and trends in the new space.

2. Assess Existing Resources:

  - Evaluate your current capabilities and resources to determine compatibility with the new venture.

3. Diversify Strategically:

  - Choose niches or products that align with your brand and existing customer base.

  - Look for synergies that allow you to leverage your strengths.

4. Test the Waters:

  - Start with a pilot or small-scale launch to gauge market response.

  - Collect feedback and adapt your approach based on initial results.

5. Build Cross-Selling Opportunities:

  - Identify opportunities for cross-selling between existing and new products or niches.

  - Leverage your customer base to promote the expansion.

6. *Adapt Marketing Strategies

  - Tailor marketing strategies to target the specific audience of the new niche or product.

  - Utilize platforms and channels preferred by the new target market.

7. Customer Education:

   - Educate your existing customer base about the new offerings.

   - Emphasize the value and benefits of the expanded range.

8. Supply Chain Considerations:

   - Ensure your supply chain can support the increased demand and different product requirements.

   - Establish reliable partnerships with suppliers in the new niche.

9. Digital Presence Expansion:

   - Update your website and online platforms to showcase the new products or niches.

   - Optimize SEO to attract relevant traffic for the expanded offerings.

10. Monitor and Iterate:

   - Continuously monitor performance metrics and customer feedback.

   - Iterate your strategies based on real-time data to optimize the expansion.

11. Risk Mitigation:

   - Identify potential risks associated with the expansion and develop mitigation plans.

   - Stay agile to adapt to unforeseen challenges.

Expanding thoughtfully into new niches or products can open up new revenue streams and enhance the overall resilience of your business.

BUILDING RELATIONSHIPS WITH MERCHANTS AND OTHER AFFILIATES

Building strong relationships with merchants and affiliates is crucial for success in affiliate marketing. Here are key strategies:

1. Open Communication:

   - Maintain transparent and open communication with merchants and affiliates.

   - Regularly update them on your promotional strategies and performance.

2. Establish Trust:

   - Demonstrate reliability and consistency in your marketing efforts.

   - Uphold your commitments and deadlines.

3. Personalized Approach:

   - Tailor your communication to the specific needs and goals of each merchant or affiliate.

   - Show genuine interest in their products or services.

4. Networking Events:

   - Attend industry events, conferences, or webinars to network with merchants and affiliates.

   - Face-to-face interactions can strengthen relationships.

5. Provide Value

   - Offer valuable insights or data that can benefit merchants or affiliates.

   - Showcase how your marketing efforts contribute to their success.

6. Negotiate Win-Win Deals:

   - Collaborate on mutually beneficial terms, ensuring both parties gain value.

   - Be flexible and willing to adjust terms based on performance.

7. Affiliate Contests or Incentives:

   - Organize contests or incentive programs to motivate affiliates.

   - Recognize and reward top-performing partners.

8. Affiliate Training:

   - Provide educational resources or training sessions for affiliates to optimize their marketing strategies.

   - Help them understand the best ways to promote products.

9. Feedback Loops:

   - Establish feedback mechanisms to continuously improve collaboration.

   - Seek input from affiliates and merchants on ways to enhance the partnership.

10. Long-Term Relationship Focus:

   - Aim for long-term relationships rather than short-term gains.

   - Invest time and effort in nurturing connections for sustained success.

11. Legal Clarity:

   - Clearly define terms and expectations in contractual agreements.

   - Ensure legal clarity to avoid misunderstandings.

Building and maintaining positive relationships with merchants and affiliates not only boosts your current affiliate marketing efforts but also sets the foundation for future collaborations and business growth

DIVERSIFYING INCOME STERAMS FOR LONG-TERM SUSTAINABILITY

Diversifying income streams is crucial for long-term sustainability. Consider these strategies:

1. Multiple Affiliate Programs:

   - Partner with various affiliate programs in different niches.

   - Spread your revenue sources across multiple products and industries.

2. Create Your Products:

  - Develop and sell your own products or services.

  - This provides direct control over pricing and enhances brand recognition.

3. Digital Products:

  - Offer digital products like e-books, online courses, or software.

  - These scalable products can generate passive income.

4. Subscription Models:

  - Implement subscription-based services for recurring revenue.

  - Examples include memberships, subscription boxes, or premium content.

5. Ad Revenue:

  - Monetize your website or platform through display advertising.

  - Platforms like Google AdSense can be a starting point.

6. Consulting or Coaching:

  - Share your expertise through consulting or coaching services.

  - Offer personalized solutions to clients or businesses.

7. Freelancing:

  - Freelance in your niche to diversify income.

  - Use platforms like Upwork or Fiverr to find additional projects.

8. Investments:

  - Explore investment opportunities, such as stocks, real estate, or other assets.

  - Diversify your portfolio to mitigate risk.

9. Affiliate Marketing Consultancy:

   - Offer consultancy services to businesses looking to improve their affiliate marketing.

   - Share your expertise and insights.

10. Podcasting or Video Content:

   - Monetize through sponsorships, ads, or listener/viewer support.

   - Platforms like Patreon can help create a steady income.

11. E-commerce Ventures:

   - Start an online store selling physical products.

   - Use platforms like Shopify or Amazon for e-commerce.

12. Partnerships and Collaborations:

   - Collaborate with other influencers or businesses for joint ventures.

   - Pool resources and expand your reach.

13. Real Estate Ventures:

   - Explore real estate opportunities for rental income or property appreciation.

   - Real estate crowdfunding is a modern option.

14. Create a Membership Site:

   - Offer premium content or community access through a membership site.

   - Generate recurring revenue from subscribers.

Diversifying income streams not only provides financial stability but also protects against market fluctuations and changes in consumer behavior. Continuously assess and adjust your strategy to adapt to evolving trends and opportunities.

CONCLUSION

In conclusion, the journey to long-term sustainability through diversified income streams is within your grasp. Embrace the opportunities that align with your skills, passions, and expertise. Take that first step toward creating multiple revenue channels, whether through affiliate marketing, your own products, consulting, or investments.

Remember, the path to success involves learning, adapting, and persevering. The diverse landscape of income streams not only safeguards against uncertainties but also opens doors to new possibilities and growth.

So, seize the moment, leverage your strengths, and embark on this journey towards financial resilience. Your commitment and proactive approach today will lay the foundation for a more secure and prosperous tomorrow. Don't just dream about it—take action now!

ENCOURAGEMENTS FOR YOU TO TAKE ACTION

To all aspiring affiliate marketers, remember that success is not a destination; it's a journey of continuous learning and adaptation. Embrace challenges as opportunities, and view setbacks as stepping stones toward growth.

In the dynamic world of affiliate marketing, persistence is your greatest ally. Stay curious, stay innovative, and stay committed to refining your strategies. The path may have its twists and turns, but each experience brings valuable lessons that propel you forward.

Believe in your potential, trust the process, and dare to dream big. Your dedication to mastering the art of affiliate marketing can transform not just your financial landscape but also your entire professional journey.

As you navigate this exciting realm, keep in mind: every click, every conversion, and every setback is a part of your success story. So, go ahead, launch those campaigns, build those connections, and let your passion fuel your progress.

The affiliate marketing world awaits your unique contributions. Seize the opportunities, overcome the challenges, and watch your efforts blossom into a thriving and fulfilling affiliate marketing career. Best of luck on your journey!